Sailing Endeavour

with *Instructive Text* by
Peter Petroff & John Ferguson

and *Imaginative Photographs* by
Rod McLeod

and *Imaginative Photographs* by

an *Introduction* by
Bruce Stannard

including *Helpful Extracts*
from the journal of
James Cook, Navigator

Proudly Sponsored by
Driza-Bone

MARITIME HERITAGE PRESS, SYDNEY
in association with
HALSTEAD PRESS

Acknowledgements

The publishers wish to acknowledge: John Maguire, Managing Director of Driza-Bone Pty Ltd for Driza-Bone's generous sponsorship of this book; Andrew Halsall for the aerial photograph on pages 56 and 57; Mike Lefroy, John Longley and Ray Parkin for their advice; and the following publications, *Captain Cook in Australia*, edited by A.W. Reed, A.H. & A.W. Reed, 1969 and *Seamanship in the Days of Sail* by John Harland, Conway Maritime Press.1985

First published in 1994 by
Maritime Heritage Press Pty Ltd
in association with
Halstead Press Pty Ltd
19A Boundary Street,
Rushcutters Bay NSW 2011

© Copyright 1994: *Text*, Peter Petroff and John Ferguson
Photographs, Rod McLeod

National Library of Australia
Cataloguing-in-Publication Data

Petroff, Peter, 1954–

Sailing Endeavour.

ISBN 1 875684 05 0

1. Cook, James, 1728–1779 – Diaries. 2. Endeavour (Ship : Replica). 3. Sailing ships – Reproductions – Great Britain. 4. Sailing ships – Great Britain – Design and construction. 1. Ferguson, John, 1937– . II. Cook, James, 1728–1779. III. Title.

623.812043

Designed by John Ferguson
Typeset by Ian MacArthur and Adtype Pty Ltd
Printed by Southbank Pacific, Melbourne

Contents

James Cook, Navigator

"I, who had the ambition not only to go farther than any man had ever been before, but as far as it was possible for man to go..."

Lt. James Cook, 1770

On Whitby's weathered West Cliff, a saltsea-stained sculpture of Captain James Cook stands forever gazing out over the bleak, grey North Sea approaches to the ancient Yorkshire port. With rolled charts tucked firmly under his left arm and a pair of dividers gripped in this scarred right hand, the hatless bronze Cook, mute yet eloquent, captures perfectly the restless, questing spirit of the man who in Charles Darwin's words, *"added a hemisphere to the civilised world"* and in the process became the greatest seaman and navigator we have ever known. On the statue's stone plinth are the final words from Alfred Lord Tennyson's Ulysses, an epitaph that speaks succinctly of Cook's brief but brilliant career: *"To strive, to seek, to find and not to yield."* Like Ulysses, the hero of Homer's epic, Cook was a man of outstanding wisdom, resourcefulness, courage and endurance. Like Ulysses too, Cook was *"to follow Knowledge like a sinking star, Beyond the utmost bounds of human thought."*

James Cook's English contemporaries called him "the most moderate, humane, gentle circumnavigator who ever went upon discoveries" ... "the ablest and most renown Navigator this or any country hath produced." And so he was. In his three great world-girdling voyages between 1768 and 1779, Cook accurately charted both islands of New Zealand, charted and took possession for Britain of some 2,000 miles of Australia's eastern coastline, penetrated deep inside the Antarctic ice, discovered the Hawaiian islands and charted the treacherous west coast of North America for over 6,000 miles from what is now Oregon to beyond the Bering Strait.

Cook served as a Royal Navy officer for only 11 years and yet he discovered more about the Pacific, the South Atlantic, the southern Indian and the Arctic and Antarctic Oceans than had been seen or imagined by all other navigators in the preceding two and a half centuries. In doing so Cook helped defeat scurvy, established precise navigation as a common sea skill and changed the face of the Pacific from the world's great abode of myths and mystery to the map we know today. While Cook holds a very special place in Australian history, he also is one of the central figures in the history of New Zealand, Canada and a host of island nations scattered throughout the Pacific. And it was, of course, his epic first voyage in the converted Whitby-built collier, *Endeavour*, which paved the way for the European settlement of Australia.

Today, thanks to many hundreds of thousands of hours of shipyard craftsmanship and unlogged years of devotion from scores of volunteers, an exact replica of *Endeavour* plies the seas. Built in Fremantle, she has evolved into a living creature, a vessel imbued with a presence which is immediately obvious to anyone who sees her.

The Endeavour project involved men and women from all walks of life and all parts of the nation, drawn together by a desire to make their own personal contribution to this once-in-a-lifetime project, the creation of a great national icon. Now that she is under sail, voyaging from port to port, *Endeavour* will become a powerful national symbol as Australia's Flagship. The central idea behind the ship is that she should reach out to Australians wherever they may be and take to them the extraordinary story of our maritime heritage.

In James Cook and *Endeavour*, Australia is blessed with exceptionally powerful symbols of courage, tenacity, skill, endurance and leadership — qualities that led to dramatic triumphs over adversity — images that today speak to us across the centuries with a singular eloquence. The very name *Endeavour* embodies the essence of a once much vaunted Australian credo: Have A Go! This indefatigable spirit characterised James Cook's life and led him to discover and chart virtually the entire eastern coast of Australia in 1770, setting Australia's history on the path it has followed to this day.

Bruce Stannard

Rain, Wind & Spray

Wet weather gear that protects today's sailors against howling gales and the unrelenting spray of the southern oceans had its origins on the tall ships which plied these same waters in the days of sail. Driza–Bones were first made by a Scot, Edward Le Roy, who discovered that torn sails made excellent wet weather gear when painted with a mixture of oils and fashioned into long sturdy coats and sou'westers. Before this canny invention, sailors would smear themselves, their clothes and even their hair with a mixture of oils or grease to ward off cold and to keep out the rain. This kept them moderately dry though somewhat uncomfortable, because clothes weighed down with several applications of grease and oil became cumbersome and quite dangerous when climbing the rigging.

When eventually Le Roy's sailors chose a life ashore they took their trusty wet weather gear with them. Their coats were soon adopted by the Australian settlers, and so popular were they on the land that they became known as Driza–Bones after the parched bones of dead animals in the arid outback.

Now the Driza–Bone has returned to its origins. There have been improvements to the coat's oiling process over time, but it is still made from natural cotton and the essential style of the Driza–Bone remains

unchanged. As well the traditional long coats and sou'westers, the crew of *Endeavour* now has a range of wet or windy weather clothes that their predecessors would envy. For those who climb aloft in the rigging, Driza–Bone short coats or oilskin parkas and trousers provide freedom to manoeuvre; sleeveless oilskin vests ward off the ocean spray, and the traditional long coat and sou'wester are still sought after by all on deck from captain to cabin boy.

Catharine Retter

The Weather Deck

he weather deck as the name implies, is the upper deck and is described in three sections. The foremost part is the fore deck or fo'c'sle; the middle part is the waist or upper deck, and the stern is known as the after deck or quarterdeck. The ship is manned from the weather deck, orders being given by the captain to the mates and from them to the topmen and thence to the crew, who are organised into four "watches". These are, from forward, fo'c'sle watch, foremast, mainmast and mizen. Over 200 lines are cleated to the weather deck for the control of spars and sails. These are laid out in a logical manner following the practice of Navy ships of the eighteenth century, each side being basically a mirror of the other.

The ship is steered from the wheel on the after deck with a lookout posted at all times on the bowsprit accompanied by a runner to report when necessary to the helm. The photographs show the main features of the weather deck from the tiller, wheel, binnacles, guns and swivel guns, to the capstan, belfry, windlass, anchors and so on. From the massive "rough-tree" rails to the many handmade blocks, to the intricate rope work, to the precise joinery, to the hand forged ironwork to the neatest whipping on the end of a line, the superb craftsmanship that created *Endeavour* is obvious everywhere.

The weather deck of the original *Endeavour* would have been somewhat more chaotic than that of today, for as Joseph Banks remarked in his journal:

> "...*our live stock consists of 17 sheep, 4 or 5 fowls, as many as S.Sea hogs, 4 or 5 muscovy ducks, an English boar, and a sow with a litter of piggs...*"

They also carried a goat for milk, the most travelled goat in history, for when Cook acquired it, it had just returned from circumnavigating the globe with Captain Wallis in the *Dolphin*.

Opposite: *Looking forward on the port side of the weather deck from the mizen channel. It was from the fore channels that the lead line was cast for sounding.*

The tiller, a five metre baulk of karri, showing the lines which lead from it through turning blocks to the drum on the wheel. Note the extension to carry over the chimney from the great cabin fireplace.

Opposite: *The steering position which shows the wheel with binnacles each side. These house the steering compasses and other instruments. Forward of the wheel is the skylight over the officers' mess. This is removed when the capstan is in use.*

April 1770

Thursday, 19th *In the P.M. had fresh gales at S.S.E. and Cloudy Squally Weather, with a large Southerly Sea; at six took in Topsails, and at 1 A.M. brought too and Sounded, but had no ground with 130 fathoms of line. At 5, set the Topsails close reef'd, and 6, saw land extending N.E. to W., distance 5 or 6 Leagues, having 80 fathoms, fine sandy bottom. We continued standing to the Westward with the Wind at S.S.W. until 8, at which time we got Topgallant Yards a Cross, made all sail, and bore away along the shore N.E. for the Easternmost land we had in sight, being at this time in the latitude of 37°58'S. and long. of 210°39'W.. The Southernmost point of land we had in sight,... I have named it Point Hicks, because Lieutenant Hicks was the first who discovered this land...*

Top: *A crewman covers his ears as the port cannon fires. These are replica cannon and are exact copies of the original* Endeavour *weapons recovered from Endeavour Reef in 1969. They are four pounders, the weight of the ball they fired. They were built for* Endeavour *by ADI (Australian Defence Industries).*

Bottom: *Heaving on the capstan bars. This is used for moving heavy gear and anchors, or to help in moving the ship around an anchorage. Traditionally a crewman sat on the centre of the capstan to assist the working rhythm of the crew by singing sea shanties.*

The "best bower" anchor is secured for sailing. These iron anchors are exact replicas of the originals, but are cast rather than forged. Note the woven rope mat for seating the fluke on the rail.

Opposite top: *The ship's beautifully cast brass bell hangs in the belfry.*

A crewman takes a turn around the windlass with the stream anchor cable preparatory to hauling in. The windlass is mounted between the carrick heads, delicately carved from solid jarrah.

Opposite bottom: *The foredeck showing the bowsprit and its extension, the jib boom. The large timber projecting forward is the cathead from which the anchor is raised and lowered. The Union flag flies from the jackstaff whilst the ship is at anchor. Note the swivel gun mounted on the starboard side.* Endeavour *carried eight swivel guns as part of her protective armament.*

Next page: *A view of the weather deck from the foretop looking aft.*

Masts & Spars

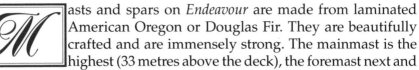asts and spars on *Endeavour* are made from laminated American Oregon or Douglas Fir. They are beautifully crafted and are immensely strong. The mainmast is the highest (33 metres above the deck), the foremast next and the mizen the lowest. They are made in three sections known as the lower mast, the topmast (which overlaps the mainmast) and the topgallant mast (which overlaps the topmast). Note the wooldings around the masts, traditionally used to strap together the pieces which form them, somewhat like the hoops around a barrel. Projecting from the bow is the bowsprit corresponding to a fourth mast, with its extension, the jib boom.

The layout of the yards to which the sails are attached can be seen in the sail plan on page 40. Each derives its name from the mast to which it belongs, mainyard, main topgallant yard, mizen topsail yard and so on. The yardarm is the outer extremity beyond which the braces and lifts are attached.

Extra sail area is achieved by the fitting of stunsail booms to the fore and main course yards. They are about half the length of their respective yards and are hauled out when in use. Originally called steering sails, these are believed to date back to Francis Drake's time and were thought to be used in light airs to maintain steerage way.

Opposite: *Taken from the foretop; crew are on the main course yard furling the sail. They gain some support from the stunsail booms mounted above the yard. One of the starboard cannons has just fired.*

April 1770

Wednesday, 18th. *Winds Southerly, a hard gale, with heavy squalls, attended with Showers of rain and a great Sea from the same Quarter. At 3 p.m. Close Reeft the Topsails, handed the main and Mizen Topsail, and got down Top Gallant Yards.At 6 the gale increased to such a height as to oblige us to take in the Foretopsail and Mainsail, and to run under the Foresail and Mizen all night; Sounding every 2 hours, but found no ground with 120 fathoms. At 6 a.m. set the Mainsail, and soon after the foretopsail, and before Noon the Main topsail, both close reeft.*

Opposite: *Looking up the mainmast to the maintop. The mizen staysail is in the foreground. Crew are climbing over the futtock shrouds onto the top.*

Next page: *The bowsprit with fore topmast staysail set. Notice the sheet and its purchase. The lookout sits comfortably on the furled jib. The bower anchor stock is visible to the right of the cathead.*

The base of the mainmast showing wooldings and the massive jeer falls which raise the course yards and hold them in position aloft.

Opposite: *Main course yard showing stunsail boom, lifts and braces. Crew working on yards attach safety harness to safety lines which are a prerequisite to pass modern safety standards.*

Next page: *Foremast, mainmast and mizen with square sails furled and staysails set.*

The Rigging

In rigging *Endeavour* about 40 kilometres of rope was used. It has all been made to the original specifications on a 140 year old rope walk. There are two types of rigging; standing rigging, which supports the masts, and running rigging which controls the yards and sails. Standing rigging needs occasional adjustment, especially when new, to take up any slack from stretching.

Standing Rigging

The stays support the masts, running forward and are named after the masthead they support, main stay, fore stay, topgallant stay and so on. The staysails are named after the stay onto which they are attached or "bent".

The shrouds give lateral support, the lower shrouds being set up from the channels which project from the sides giving greater sideways support. Backstays, as the name implies, assist in keeping tension against the stays. The bobstay holds the bowsprit down. Along each yard the footropes are attached to support crew working aloft.

Running Rigging

A great many lines control all aspects of the rig. Some of these lines are:
Halliards (haul yards) which raise the yards into position and take most of the weight. Lifts control the yards in the vertical plane. Braces haul the yards from side to side. Yards are thus moved under control at all times, one brace being hauled on whilst its opposite is being eased off. Halliards also haul the staysails up along their stays. The staysails are controlled by sheets, ropes attached to the corner of the sail. Other lines to control the sails are known as clewlines, buntlines, bowlines, reeflines, brails and gaskets, and may be identified in the photographs.

Opposite: *A crewman going aloft on the starboard ratlines. Note that his hands hold the shrouds, whilst his feet use the ratlines, a precaution from the early days of sail when the ratlines were often rotten.*

August 1770

Tuesday, 7th. *Strong gales at S.E., S.E. by S., and S.S.E.,
with cloudy weather at Low water in the P.M. I and several of
the officers kept a look out at the Mast head to see for a
Passage between the Shoals…*

*After having well viewed our situation from the Mast Head, I
saw that we were surrounded on every side with Dangers, in
so much that I was quite at a loss which way to steer when the
weather will permit us to get under sail, for to beat back to the
S.E. the way we came, as the Master would have had me done,
would be an endless piece of work, as the winds blow
constantly from that Quarter, and very Strong, without
hardly any intermission; on the other hand, if we do not find a
passage to the Northward we shall have to come back at last.
At 11 the Ship drove, and obliged us to bear away to a Cable
and one third, which brought us up again; but in the morning
the Gale increasing, she drove again. This made us let go the
Small Bower Anchor, and bear away a whole Cable on it and 2
on the other; and even after this she still kept driving slowly,
until we had got down Top gallant masts, struck Yards and
Top masts close down, and made all snug; then she rid fast…*

Opposite: *The shrouds are made up of lines hauled tight by laniards rove
through wooden deadeyes. The lower deadeyes are held out by the channels
which are linked to the hull by iron chain plates.*

Following pages:
Left: *The mainmast heart is seized around the bowsprit. It is made from
Western Australian tuart.*

Right: *Mainstay and preventer stay with staysail bent on. Preventer stays
provide a margin of safety by giving support if the mainstay gives way.*

Opposite: *A crewman has collapsed a coil by taking it off its belaying pin in readiness to ease the line. Correct coiling and belaying of lines is of great importance in handling the gear efficiently and safely.*

Next page: *A mass of truss tackles and jeer falls at the base of the foremast. The jeers raise the course yards and hold them in position.*

Left: *Crew on the spritsail topsail yard coming into port. The sails are furled and tied with gaskets. The arrangement of lifts and braces can be clearly seen.*

Right: *Crew climb up the futtock shrouds onto the top. The topmast shrouds are spread by the top to give lateral support to the mast. Tension is maintained by the futtock shrouds, which connect the top to the lower shrouds. Note the protective railing. Many a time Cook and his officers went to the top for observation.*

The Sails

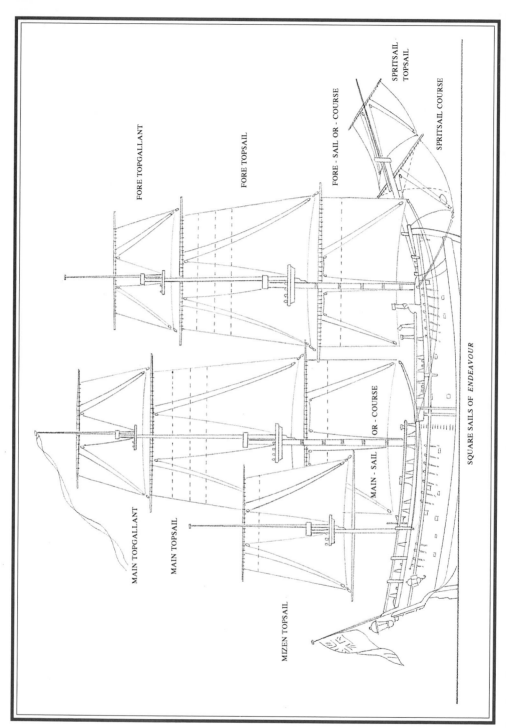

SPRITSAIL TOPSAIL

SPRITSAIL COURSE

FORE TOPGALLANT

FORE TOPSAIL

FORE - SAIL OR - COURSE

MAIN TOPGALLANT

MAIN TOPSAIL

MAIN - SAIL OR - COURSE

MIZEN TOPSAIL

SQUARE SAILS OF *ENDEAVOUR*

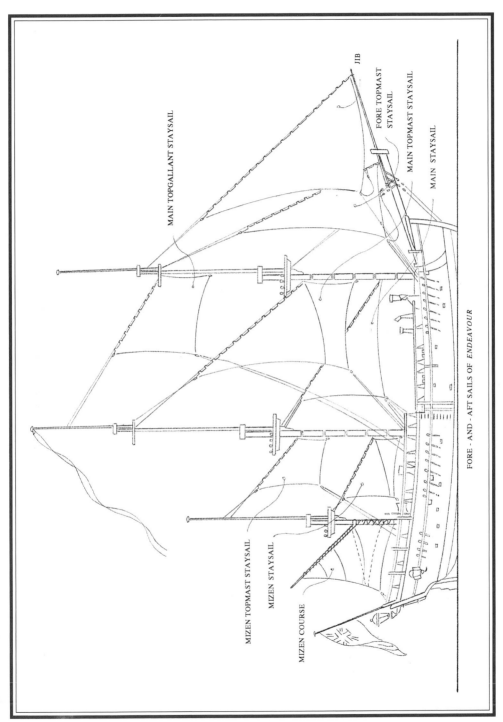

MAIN TOPGALLANT STAYSAIL

JIB

FORE TOPMAST STAYSAIL

MAIN TOPMAST STAYSAIL

MAIN STAYSAIL

MIZEN TOPMAST STAYSAIL

MIZEN STAYSAIL

MIZEN COURSE

FORE - AND - AFT SAILS OF *ENDEAVOUR*

uradon, from which the sails are made, is a synthetic canvas which looks and handles like the original flax. *Endeavour* can set 17 working sails and 9 stunsails, not necessarily all at once. They are divided into square sails, set on the yards, which drive the ship before the wind, and fore and aft sails, which assist the ship when close hauled. Although made of modern materials, *Endeavour's* sails are made in the traditional manner and handled likewise. The diagrams on the two previous pages show clearly the two types of sails with the exception of the stunsails, which are not shown. Stunsails are set on boom extensions to the yards to increase sail area when running before the wind.

The sails are controlled by lines, each of which has a specific purpose. The sheets, attached to the clew of the sail, spread the foot of the sail. The bowlines keep the weather leech taut. The clewlines haul the clews or lower corners up to the yards preparatory to furling. Buntlines are attached to the foot of the sail and haul it up for the same purpose. Reeflines pull the leech or sides of the sail up to aid reefing and furling. Brails are lines arranged to haul the mizen course up to its gaff. And finally, gaskets are lines to wrap around the furled sails to keep them secure and tidy.

Endeavour is a fine sight under full sail and in the right conditions has sailed at over 9 knots, which for a "humble collier" of 550 tonnes is pretty good going.

Opposite: Endeavour *under full sail on a port tack. The bowsprit carries the spritsail topsail and spritsail. Above them are the jib and fore topmast staysail. The foremast and mainmast carry topgallants, topsails, and courses, behind which can be seen the mizen topsail. Note the reefing points.*

Sail furling on topsail and topgallant yards. Crew are attaching gaskets, flat plaited ropes to tie the sail neatly in position. Notice the footropes.

Opposite: *The foremast with fore course and fore topsail set. The spritsail can also be seen. Crew are returning to deck. The main topmast staysail and main staysail are furled.*

Opposite: Main topsail set with crew unfurling main topgallant. The mainsail or course is ready to let go.

Main course almost set. The buntlines which hold the foot of the sail need overhauling or slackening off.

With all square sails set, plus the fore topmast staysail, and the breeze on the port quarter, Endeavour *makes a serene sight. James Cook described this as her best point of sailing.*

Opposite: *Crew aloft unfurling the main topsail. The main topmast staysail is in the foreground.*

Next page: *The mizen topsail setting well with mizen on the gaff behind it. The only mechanical advantage available is from block and tackle. There are over 700 hand made wooden blocks on* Endeavour.

Working the Ship

andling *Endeavour* is a complicated and arduous business requiring skill, co-ordination, cooperation, strength and courage. Reefing topsails in a blow is not for the faint hearted. Many of the skills in sailing square rigged ships have been passed down from sailors of an earlier era. Much has been learned also from contemporary accounts and later research on the subject. *Endeavour* is rather special in this respect, for of all the tall ships sailing in the world today, none other comes from the 18th century. It is a tribute to the captain, mates, bosuns, and crew that *Endeavour* performs so well, in fact better than expected, and that they learned to handle the ship so well in such a short time after she was launched.

Working the ship covers many activities. However the organisation of the crew is the first and most important aspect of this. Teamwork is essential, many hands making light work of bending on sails, loosing, furling, reefing, making and shortening sail at sea, and the more complicated manoeuvres of tacking and wearing (gybing). Additional skills are required for steering, navigating, anchoring and operating in heavy weather.

The crew is made up of 15 professionals, 30 voyage crew and ten supernumeraries. The professionals include a captain, two mates, engineer, navigator, bosun, four topmen, two upper topmen, two carpenters and a cook. To be selected for voyage crew, you need to be fit, healthy and willing to undertake all aspects of sailing an 18th century museum ship. Preference is given to those with sea-going square rig experience.

Opposite: *On the helm. The ship is steered from the wheel on the after deck. The helmsman checks the steering compass in the binnacle whilst the First Mate looks on. Keeping a steady course is an art which needs some practice.Today courses are steered by the compass marked in 360 degrees. In Cook's day the compass was divided into 32 points.*

[54]

The crew secure everything that could move as the sea becomes rougher. With an increasing wind over the starboard quarter the main course is full and drawing efficiently.

Opposite: *Getting ready for heavy weather, the crew furl the mizen topsail. The helmsman work in pairs for it is not light work especially in strong winds.*

Next page: Endeavour *heels to port in heavy seas with the wind at 45 knots from the south. The only sails set now are the fore topmast staysail, fore course, main staysail, main course, mizen staysail and mizen course.*

The Captain and the other officers gather in the great cabin for the daily briefing.

April 1770

Saturday, 14th. *Calm serene weather, with sometimes light Airs from the Northward. At sun set found the Variation to be 11° 28′ E., and in the morning to be 11° 30′ E. The Spritsail Topsail being wore to rags, it was condemn'd as not fit for its proper use, and Converted to repair the 2 Top Gallant Sails, they being of themselves so bad as not to be worth the Expence of new Canvas, but with the help of this sail may be made to last some time longer...*

Opposite: *Lashing the main staysail requires teamwork as does all other sail handling aboard.*

Opposite: *Sail handling and controlling the yards and halliards require the strength that a co-ordinated team can provide. Crew on the after deck haul on the main brace.*

Catting the anchor also needs a good tug-o'-war team.

June 1770

Tuesday, 12th. *Fortunately we had little wind, fine weather and a smooth sea, all this 24 hours, which in the P.M. gave us an opportunity to carry out the 2 bower anchors, one on the starboard quarter, and the other right astern, got blocks and tackles upon the cables, brought the falls in abaft and hove taut. By this time it was 5 o'clock P.M.; the tide we observed now begun to rise, and the leak increased upon us, which obliged us to set the third pump to work, as we should have done the 4th also, but could not make it work...*

The spritsail and spritsail topsail braces being hauled down to be made up on the belaying pins. Each line is taken around its pin three times before being made up and coiled. When being eased even in the dark each watch will know exactly what state the line is in.

Opposite: *With over 200 lines to handle, neatness is essential for efficient and safe operation of the whole gear. Working* Endeavour *is a ceaseless job of coiling and easing lines and furling and unfurling sails!*

Many hands are needed for working the capstan under heavy load. Note the line around the drum.

Taking in the spritsail topsail. The yard has been hauled back from its fully set position on the jib boom.

Opposite: *Crew apply tension to the main staysail sheet.*

Handling the anchors is not light work. Here the crew have raised the stream anchor and are securing it or "catting the anchor". The crewman at the top is standing on one of the "seats of ease" as the original toilet seat was called. Not much comfort or privacy here for crews in the 18th century.

Opposite: *The anchor securely catted. Note the carved crown on the end of the cathead.*

Following page: *An upper topman looks on as the lookout seats himself on the furled jib whilst his runner tidies lines on the fore deck. Watch crew are rotated in the duties to be done. Driza-Bone wet weather gear protects the crew against cold and wet squally weather.*

Make & Mend

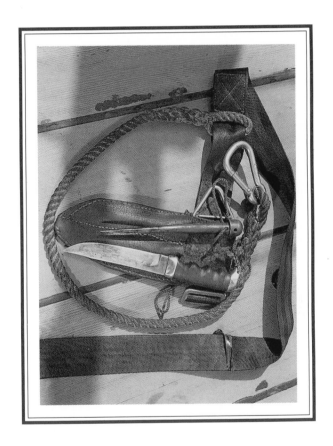

ames Cook's journal contains frequent references to maintenance work on *Endeavour*. Nothing has changed. A square rigged wooden ship needs constant attention especially if it is to be maintained in a safe condition; to say nothing of prolonging its beauty.

Rope and rigging work, carpentry, caulking, painting, coating the rigging with Stockholm tar, cleaning the decks and taking care of sails, are just some of the never-ending jobs to be done. *Endeavour's* crew gain great satisfaction from doing these jobs properly, in a manner little changed over the centuries.

Opposite: *Repairing ratlines on the main shrouds. Note the use of the traditional canvas bucket and rigger's tools.*

July 1770

Saturday, 7th. *Fresh breezes at S.E. and fair weather. Employ'd getting on board Coals, Ballast, etc., and caulking the Ship; a work that could not be done while she lay aground. The Armourer and his Mate are still employ'd at the forge making and repairing sundry Articles in the Iron way.*

Opposite: *The bosun finishes an eye splice using a palm and needle. All rigging work is done by hand using traditional methods.*

Following pages:
Top: *A ship's carpenter working in the foc's'le.*

Bottom: *Happy hour! Holy stoning the decks in the officers quarters. This job was traditionally done on Sundays and as the abrasive blocks were the size of bibles, they were known as holy stones.*

Right: *A ship's carpenter repairs the caulking on a deck seam on the weather deck. The caulking is a pitch mix and in hot weather must be kept cool by hosing down or it tends to melt and become sticky.*

Left: *Making an ocean plait, a rope mat often used to stop chafing.*

Right: *Coiling and stowing spare lines.* Endeavour *uses a combination of natural and synthetic cordage.*

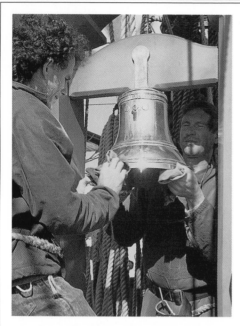

Left: *Polishing the ship's bell is a daily event. Traditionally the bell sounded every half hour of a four hour watch.*

Right: *The canvas bucket is used for hauling water. Unlike solid buckets it does not damage the ship's sides.*

Opposite: *A topman sailmaker with palm and needle stitches a sail bag. Endeavour's carpenter's shop and sail locker contain a full complement of tools for maintaining the ship at sea.*

A back A sail is a back when the wind strikes the forward surface

A-lee When the tiller is on the lee side

Aloft Up in the rigging or on the yards

Anchor a-weigh The anchor is no longer on the bottom

Anchor is catted The anchor is hanging from the cathead

Anchor

Bowers   the two biggest anchors

Stream   the next largest anchor

Kedges   the smaller anchors stowed below

Brails Lines used to gather in the mizen course

Bunt The middle part of a square sail or the forward part of a quadrangular sail

Buntlines Ropes attached to the foot of the sail to haul it up

By the wind, close hauled and **full and by** All terms used to describe a ship sailing as close to the wind as possible

Capstan Device for hauling up heavy objects or hauling in lines. On some ships it is used to haul up the anchor

Cat block Large double block for hauling up the anchor to the cathead

Cathead Large piece of timber overhanging the bow used to draw the anchor into position

Cat hairpins Short lengths of rope seized to the upper part of the lower shrouds and futtock staves

Channels Broad pieces of wood projecting out from the side of the hull to support the dead-eyes

Cleats Pieces of wood to fasten ropes to

Close hauled *see* **By the wind**

Conning Directing the helmsman how to steer

Davit Large piece of timber used to fish the anchor on board

Deadeye A block with three holes in it to rove the laniard through

Ear rings Small ropes to make fast the upper corners of square sails

Ease off Slacken

Eye of the wind The direction from which the wind blows

Fathom Old measurement of depth equal to 6 feet or 1.8288 metres

Fid A tapered piece of wood or iron generally used for splicing ropes; a piece of iron which supports the topmast and prevents it from falling through to the trestle trees

Flukes The broad parts or palms of the anchor

Fo'c'sle Forward raised part of the upper deck

Full and by *see* **By the wind**

Furling Making fast the sails to the yards by the gaskets

Gangway Ramp to enter the ship by

Gasket A piece of plaited rope to tie the sails to the yards

Halliards Ropes used to hoist sails or yards

Hand Another expression for taking in sail

Heel To incline to one side

Head to wind When the ship's bow is pointing into the wind

Helm A large piece of wood connected to the rudder (tiller); this is connected by tiller ropes to the wheel

Horse A rope fastened to the yard for the crew to stand on

Laniard Short length of rope to prevent loss of an object overboard; to set shrouds taut with dead eyes

Jewel blocks Blocks hanging from the extremities of the topsail yard

Larboard The old term for the port or left side

League Old measurement of distance, 3 miles or 5 kilometres

Leeward The opposite side to that from which the wind is blowing

Leeway Movement of the ship to leeward

Lubber A sailor who does not know his duty

Man the yards To send crew up on the yards

Port The left hand side

Rattle down the shrouds To fix the ratlines to the shrouds

Ratlines Short pieces of rope tied between shrouds to act as rungs for climbing aloft

Reef Reduce a sail's area by tying it to the yards using the reefing points

Rig Fit the rigging to the masts

Round in Brace the yards more square

Serve Wind rope (marlin) around another rope to prevent chafe

Sound Find the bottom by using a lead line

Starboard The right hand side

Steer Manage the ship by movement of the helm

Tack Change course by passing the bow of the ship through the eye of the wind

Waist of a ship The part between the main and fore drifts

Wake The track left by the ship on the water

Wear (Gybing) To change course with the wind over the stern

Watch Division of the ship's company who keep the deck

Way of the ship Her progress through the water

Yard Spar setting across a mast and normally used to support a sail